Optimal Health

With Banchory Spinal Health

Felicity Crone

BSc Chiro DC, LRCC, IBCLC

Typesetting and page layout by Ashdown Creative
www.ashdowncreative.co.uk

DISCLAIMER

The book is for informational purposes only. Neither the publisher nor the author is engaged in rendering professional advice or services to the individual reader. The ideas, procedures and suggestions contained in this book are not intended as a substitute for consulting with your medical professional. All matters regarding your health require medical supervision. Neither the author nor the publisher shall be liable or responsible for any loss or damage allegedly arising from any information or suggestion in this book.

While the author has made every effort to provide accurate information at the time of publication, neither the publisher nor the author assumes any responsibility for errors or for changes that occur after publication. Further, the publisher does not have any control over and does not assume any responsibility for author or third-party websites or their content.

DEDICATION

This book is dedicated to my wonderful team, who enrich my life and make my "work" feel like a grand day out. I know that anyone who reads this and comes into our clinic will learn to love my team as much as I do.

ACKNOWLEDGMENTS

To all of our Chiropractors, Osteopaths, Massage therapists and other practitioners, Clinic Assistants and Practice Manager – past and present – your hands and incredible skills have helped create a better world, long may this continue!

To our patients – looking after you is the greatest honour and why we do what we do. Thank you for putting your trust in our hands, we are nothing without you.

Contents

Banchory Spinal Health

In 2012, Felicity bought her very first chiropractic bench with every penny she had. Since then, Banchory Spinal Health has grown to a huge practice serving thousands of people every year, becoming the largest spinal health clinic in Scotland.

Our dedicated team of practitioners are the best in their fields, and we are proud to look after you to help you achieve more from life with a healthy, happy body.

Thank you for choosing us and trusting us to look after you.

www.banchoryspinalhealth.co.uk

Foreword

Health is a spectrum.

We welcome many through our doors in pain and dysfunction, living their lives in a struggling state, far from the vital human beings they once were. It is our goal to use hands-on chiropractic, osteopathy and massage therapy to reconnect your body to itself.

Restoration of function and reduction in pain is, however, just the beginning. Health "is not merely the absence of disease" or pain; but rather living in a state of maximised potential and optimised function, and this is our purpose:

> We are a highly motivated and caring team who are here to support our community to achieving optimal health. It is our mission to inspire you to live a life of freedom and vitality.
>
> We are committed to our patients and are dedicated to maintaining our standard of excellence.
>
> Anyone who steps into our clinic becomes part of our family as we welcome all ages into our care.

Our first clinic opened in 2012, and since then we have seen literally thousands of people who need our help. What is amazing to me is just how unhealthy many of us are, even though the majority of us understand the basics about how to stay healthy. When our bodies are struggling with ill health, it doesn't take much for normal day-to-day life to become very difficult! It's of no surprise to me that this may then result in pain in some area of our bodies.

If you are suffering with pain and need help ASAP – the next section is for you!

A Bad Day

It is important that we address first things first. By this I mean it's likely that you are in pain if you are reading this book. Before we go into everything else that is required for optimal health. I want to talk about easy things you can do to help yourself NOW if you are struggling in pain, before you meet us in person.

Have you ever had a bad day?

You know what I mean... it's probably the reason you sought our help in the first place.

So what should you do if you're having a bad day?

ICE

We will almost always recommend ice for an acute flare up of pain. This is because it is very likely that there will be an increase in inflammation of the area. Ice has been shown to reduce that inflammation, which may ease off some of the pain.

We recommend that when you are in acute pain, you pop an icepack on the area for 10 mins, and repeat every hour as needed.

Important: Never put an icepack on your bare skin! Always use a tea towel or layer of clothing, you would not believe how many people "burn" their skin with ice packs.

Although a bag of frozen peas will have the same effect, we always recommend a proper icepack that will remain flexible even when frozen, they are very durable and will last you for years.

KEEP MOVING

The last thing that we recommend for acute musculoskeletal pain is bed-rest. This is out-dated information and studies have shown that it will probably extend the length of time that you are in severe pain. It will also lead to what we call "de-conditioning", which basically means your joints and muscles become weaker, so when you go to resume your daily activities after your pain subsides, you may be more likely to injure yourself again.

When in pain, we recommend you try to move around often and don't remain still for longer than 30 mins except to go to bed. Try to do at least two lots of 30 minute walks per day, even more than that if you can manage. At this stage little and often is best. Keep your walks to a flat surface and no climbing up any hills, you don't want to get stuck at the top!

STAYING HYDRATED

It is well known to us that most people don't drink enough water. We will cover this in more detail later on in the book, but as an important short-term measure for managing pain, it is very important to keep your water levels topped up.

Our bodies are mostly water – the discs in your spine are 80% water! The disc's ability to be a great shock absorber is dependent on its hydration level.

By the time you are feeling thirsty you are already very dehydrated, so for your back's sake – get at least 2 litres per day. This will also help keep you from sitting still for too long!

RELAXING

Stress plays a huge part in the development of pain. Again, we will cover this in more depth shortly, however it's worth mentioning now as well. Over the time that our practice has been around we have seen thousands of patients in pain, and we have never ever seen anyone having a VERY BAD DAY pain-wise who isn't also suffering with some degree of stress. The research is starting to catch up with what is already obvious to us – stress causes your body to function differently; your muscles become tighter, your joints become less flexible and your body goes into fight or flight mode. This makes you more susceptible to injury and pain.

Now you are with us, you can relax knowing that we are here to look after you. We have a collection of experts here to make sure you become well again and STAY WELL.

The Problem With Our Modern Healthcare System

"I think the biggest problem with healthcare today is not its cost – which is a big problem – but for all that money, it's not an expression of our humanity."

JONATHAN BUSH

"Government doesn't solve problems – it subsidises them."

RONALD REAGAN

The biggest problems in the modern healthcare system throughout the world are the same: high costs, poor results, frequent medical errors, and patient dissatisfaction.[1] Simultaneously, we face a global epidemic of obesity and chronic disease. For example, cardiovascular disease, diabetes, dementia and Alzheimer disease were the leading causes of death in the UK in 2020.[2]

The structure of the modern healthcare system was set up at the beginning of the 20th century. It gave more importance to an acute care approach and much less priority to prevention and public health. The main emphasis was on understanding and treating infectious diseases and reliance on laboratory research.[3]

This strategy made sense 100 years ago because of the prevalence of acute infectious diseases in a young population. However, it doesn't make as much sense now. With the ageing of the population, the burden of disease has shifted toward chronic diseases. The most common causes of death are now obesity and smoking, which result in delayed but progressive disease.[4] Even during COVID-19 in the developed world, chronic diseases are outstripping acute infectious diseases.[5]

The main feature of modern healthcare is its use of a disjointed, task-based system that is aimed at addressing acute symptoms. It takes notice only after asymptomatic people become diseased and require drug treatment. This system favours speciality over primary care and medication or surgical procedures over lifestyle changes.

Moreover, the modern healthcare system relies on new and costly technology and pharmaceuticals, even if their benefits are not clearly understood. Many preventive and cost-effective strategies are not researched or adopted because they cannot be patented or made profitable.

For example, between 2014 and 2020, total health spending in the UK has grown at 2% a year on average, from £124bn to £137bn. This period has seen constraints in NHS pay growth, staffing shortages, a marked rise in waiting times and rise in NHS provider deficits because the cost of delivering healthcare has outstripped funding. As a result, funding has focussed increasingly on day-to-day spending at the expense of wider investment in the NHS.[6]

Modern medical research usually pursues isolated problems and short-term "magic bullet" solutions. Often, the model for treating acute infectious disease is applied to the treatment of chronic disease, with no thought to the bigger picture of why these problems have developed in the first place.

Changing this broken healthcare system requires alterations in medical education, medical research, health policy, and reimbursement. It is my belief that the current fragmentation of healthcare could be replaced by a patient-centred, whole-person approach. For example, the government could support research on the development and dissemination of prevention strategies. Moreover, it should reward the use of appropriate non-patentable therapies. Primary care physicians could act as health coaches and all healthcare professionals should adopt a coordinated multidisciplinary team approach.

Medical education should include prevention strategies such as healthy lifestyle choices, nutritional health, fitness and exercise, mental and emotional wellbeing and how to maintain healthy habits.

I would like to make it clear at this point – I am tremendously grateful for our national health service. When any of my family or I have an acute injury, an acute illness or infection, our health service professionals are the first people I wish to see! The need for management of acute disorders will always remain, however, positive health promotion is the only way to halt the emerging pandemic of chronic disease.[7]

Our current healthcare system is focused not on health maintenance but on the treatment of disease, which is mainly dependent on expensive drugs and invasive surgeries. The mission of the present healthcare system seems to be to maximize profits rather than helping people to maintain or regain their health.[8]

Not only is our healthcare system mediocre-to-poor, but many of us are unable to access it easily. According to a large survey conducted by the Commonwealth Fund, the quality of healthcare attitudes and experiences of people within these countries are somewhat disappointing.

The highlights of the survey are:

1. **Fewer people are receiving healthcare**
   This is due to the high cost of modern medical care.

2. **Lack of regular, timed access to a primary healthcare provider**
   Often, doctors don't know important information about the medical history of their patients, which affects the quality of medical care.

3. **Poor access to healthcare**
   For example, only 41 per cent of patients in the UK can consult a doctor on the same day that they need one. Access to after-hours medical care (early in the morning, late in the evening, and on weekends and holidays) is even more difficult. And one in six patients attending hospital A&E units had to wait longer than four hours.[9]

4. **Poor management of healthcare**
   This includes gaps in communication, duplicate testing, poor access to medical records, and violation of confidentiality.

5. **Medical errors**
   These include hospital-acquired infections, adverse drug reactions, inappropriate medical treatments, unnecessary surgeries, and operating on the wrong body part.

6. **Doctors don't listen to their patients**
   Patient satisfaction is also linked to how well their physicians explain things to them, how much time they spend with them and how well their appointments are managed.

7. **High chronic disease rates**
   This indicates a lack of attention to lifestyle habits such as diet, exercise, sleep, and stress management.

8. **Most people are dissatisfied with the current healthcare system**
   More than 15 per cent of Britons want a complete overhaul of the healthcare system. And only 26 per cent in the UK are satisfied with the present healthcare system.[10]

Some of the major problems of our healthcare system are:

1. Chronic Disease

One of the biggest health problems in the UK is **obesity**. The numbers are alarming.

- **64%** of UK adults are overweight or obese in 2017.

- Overall, **67% of men and 62% of women** are classified as overweight or obese.

- **20%** of children in Year 6 are classified as obese.

- Hospital admissions, where obesity was reported as a factor, rose 15% from 2016/17 to 711,0010,660 hospital admissions directly related to obesity in 2017/18, only 100 less than in 2016.

- **29%** of adults are obese, up from 26% in 2016.[11]

Unfortunately, the obesity epidemic has led to a more dangerous disorder: metabolic syndrome. The World Health Organisation and other medical groups, especially ATP-III, published the metabolic syndrome concept in 2002 to diagnose and treat an increased cardiometabolic risk. (It was formerly called Syndrome X.)

Metabolic syndrome consists of these five variables:

- obesity

- hyperglycemia (high blood sugar)

- hypertension (high blood pressure)

- hypertriglyceridemia (high fat levels in the blood)

- low HDL[12] (low levels of good cholesterol)

According to the National Cholesterol Education Program High Blood Cholesterol ATP III guidelines, a person has metabolic syndrome if any three of the following are present:

RISK FACTOR	DEFINING LEVEL
Abdominal obesity*	(waist circumference)
Men	>102 cm (>40 inches)
Women	>88 cm (>35 inches)
Fasting Glucose	>110 mg/dL
Blood Pressure	>130/>85 mmHg
Triglycerides	>150 mg/dL
HDL cholesterol	(mg/dL)
Men	<40 mg/dL
Women	<50 mg/dL

Risk factors for metabolic syndrome (minimum three)

*Overweight and obesity are associated with insulin resistance and metabolic syndrome. However, the presence of abdominal obesity is more highly correlated with metabolic risk factors than is an elevated body mass index (BMI). Therefore, the simple measure of waist circumference is recommended to identify the bodyweight component of metabolic syndrome.

Metabolic syndrome is increasingly common, and up to one third of UK adults have it. The presence of metabolic syndrome or any of its components indicates a greater risk of developing complications such as type 2 diabetes and heart disease. However, positive lifestyle changes can delay or even reverse the development of serious health problems.

2. The Opioid Problem

Opioids are a group of pain-relieving drugs naturally found in the opium poppy plant. They can be made from the poppy plant (morphine) or synthesized in a laboratory (fentanyl). Opioids are suitable for relieving acute pain and pain at the end of life but there is little evidence that they are helpful for long-term pain.[13]

In fact, doctors that specialise in pain have stated that there is a lack of evidence of effectiveness and the potential for harm when opioids are prescribed for long-term pain.[14]

Despite this, opioids are widely prescribed for long-term pain. Unfortunately, opioid prescribing more than doubled in the period from 1998 to 2018.[15] There is a reasonable fear of an opioid epidemic in the UK,[16] similar to the more serious opioid crisis in the USA.[17]

This clearly shows that our healthcare system is focusing on the symptom instead of the problem. Pain is just a symptom that tells us something is wrong. Pain is not the problem.

3. Mental Health Disorders

Major depression is thought to be the second leading cause of disability worldwide and a major contributor to suicide and even heart disease. Mental health in the UK is as follows:

- 1 in 6 people experienced a common mental health problem within the last week.

- 1 in 5 women are reported to have mental health problems.

- 1 in 8 men are reported to have mental health problems.

- 5,821 suicides were reported in the UK in 2017.

- 75% of these suicides in the UK were by men.[18]

In addition, dementia and Alzheimer disease were the top cause of death in the UK in 2017 (12.7% of all deaths).

4. Decline in Quality of Life

Life expectancy of British adults has been cut by six months by the Institute and Faculty of Actuaries, which calculates life expectancy on behalf of the UK pension industry. The institute said it now expects men aged 65 to die at 86.9 years (instead of 87.4 years), while women who reach 65 are likely to die at 89.2 years (instead of 89.7 years). This is the biggest reduction in official longevity forecasts. Compared with 2015, projections for life expectancy are now down by 13 months for men and 14 months for women. Some of the possible reasons are austerity and cuts in NHS spending, and worsening obesity, diabetes and dementia.[19]

Stress: According to a survey on a study group of 2000 people across Great Britain, 37% of British residents feel stressed for at least one full day per week. Women were substantially more likely to be stressed than men; they suffered from stress for three more days per month than men. The most common cause of stress was money, followed by work, health concerns, failure to get enough sleep, and the pressure of household chores.[20]

If you have a disorder that affects your health, our conventional healthcare system will prescribe a drug that will relieve or reduce your symptoms. However, that drug probably won't eliminate the underlying cause of your disorder. So you may have to continue to take the drug as long as the disorder persists and you'll also have to deal with any side effects caused by it. So although you may have a slightly improved quality of life, you will have to depend on the drug to get through each day.

On the other hand, the goal of authentic healthcare is to transform every patient from **surviving** to **thriving**, which means maximising comfort, performance and optimising your body's potential.

This ideal is in line with the World Health Organization's definition of health:

> "Health is a state of complete physical, mental and social well-being and not merely the absence of disease or infirmity."[21]

This ideal of health can be best served by personalised medicine because it offers a combination of conventional medical therapies and complementary therapies that are backed by high-quality scientific evidence for safety and effectiveness. Personalised medicine is healing-oriented medicine that takes account of the whole person, including all aspects of lifestyle. It emphasises the therapeutic relationship between practitioner and patient, is informed by evidence, and makes use of all appropriate therapies.[22]

We at Banchory Spinal Health believe in personalised healthcare so that you can achieve the highest levels of your health. When you seek care in our clinic, our goals during the initial stage are:

- Uncover the underlying cause of the health problem

- Suggest a care plan to produce the fastest results possible

- Offer ways you can participate in your recovery

- Explain the value of post-symptomatic wellness care

We help you to change the prevailing symptom-masking model of health (supressing your body's warning signs -symptoms- so you can carry on "as normal") in favour of a bespoke wellness model that suits you.

In this book, we will explain the vital principles that will help you to live a more vibrant, pain-free life! These are:

H – Hands-On Healthcare

E – Exercise

A – Attitude

L – Love your Food

T – Time

H – Hydrate

Hands-On Healthcare

"If there is a single definition of healing, it is to touch with mercy and awareness those pains from which we have withdrawn in judgment and dismay."

STEPHEN LEVINE

YOUR BODY IS A STRUCTURE

FUNCTIONAL PYRAMID

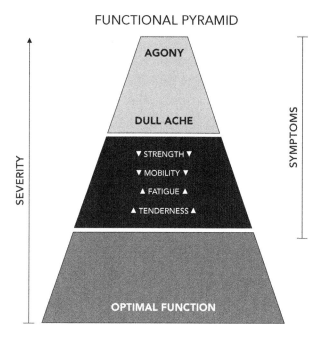

When patients attend my clinic, they are often in a lot of pain. This is to say that their symptoms have got to a point that they cannot continue their daily activities any longer. These people are at the top of the function pyramid above.

However, to get to this point, a lot of physiological changes have already occurred in your body's joints, muscles and nerves, but a lot of the time this would only manifest as a dull ache or slight stiffness, so most people are likely to ignore these changes.

So how do we get to this point?

It is fair to say that most of us these days spend far too much time sitting. Research shows that the majority of the workforce in developed countries spend nearly 8 hours per day sitting! There is a growing body of research that finds a strong correlation between prolonged sitting and elevated risk of illness and injury.[23]

Our bodies are designed to move often. Regular movement helps keep our joints lubricated, our muscles elastic and our nerves firing regularly. A sedentary lifestyle also leads to another chronic problem … poor posture.

POSTURE

Posture is something we talk about daily at Banchory Spinal Health. It is something that we very strongly feel contributes to most of the issues our patients present with. So much so that we invested in the latest posture screening technology, which uses specialised software to assess postural changes throughout your care with us.

Take a look at this picture. This is a common site across homes and offices worldwide. Imagine the position of the spine here – the lower part of the spine is curved forward, the upper part of the spine is curved forward, and the head is situated well in front of the rest of the body.

So why does poor posture lead to pain?

Did you know – our heads weigh about as much as a bowling ball? We are supposed to carry around our heads on top of our spine, with every spinal joint and muscle sharing the load evenly. However, as you can see above, when our head is sitting so far forward, some of the muscles and joints are taking all the force whilst others have completely switched off.

This results in abnormal muscular contraction. When larger muscles contract, they usually only do so for short bursts. We also have smaller muscles which are designed to help with posture, but because they are small they are not designed to take a large amount of weight. However, when these smaller postural muscles get exposed to repeated long episodes of strain, this results in ischaemia (lack of blood flow) to the muscles. This then leads to a build-up of metabolites such as lactic acid, which causes the muscle to reflexively tighten up even more, and this is when people will complain of a muscle "spasm". Which for most people is very painful and often requires medical intervention such as muscle relaxants. When the muscles get into this state, they can no longer support the spinal joints, resulting in joint strains and asymmetric joint movement, which in turn creates increased probability of problems in the future.

A similar thing occurs in the lumbar spine (the lower part) and sadly this sometimes results in the discs becoming compromised, which is a much more serious (and painful) problem.

So how do we correct our poor posture?

It is important that once you have started your care with us that we make sure the problem isn't likely to return. So our practitioners will ensure that we give you specific exercises that suit you and your particular postural problems, that you can easily integrate into your daily life. That being said, there are some easy things you can do now to improve your posture.

1. If you work in a seated position, do everything you can to move to a standing desk.

2. Take regular breaks. No amount of exercise will counteract the problems that will occur if you remain seated for 8 hours a day. The ONLY solution is to move every 30mins.

3. Be aware of your head – it should sit on top of your shoulders not in front of them!

4. If your shoulders are hunched up round your ears then RELAX and drop them down and back.

5. BREATHE! A lot of us don't breathe deeply enough. This will help blood flow to your muscles.

6. Exercise – basically the more you move the better. More on exercise later on in the book.

Once we know about your posture, we can really accurately assess whereabouts in your body we need to be working on. Our chiropractors and osteopaths have spent years (4-5 years of full-time education) training to be able to accurately diagnose a huge range of complaints, but often our patients might not know exactly what our practitioners do.

CHIROPRACTIC

"I've been going to chiropractors for as long as I can remember. It's as important to my training as practicing my swing." **TIGER WOODS**

"Look well to the spine for the cause of disease" **HIPPOCRATES**

Chiropractic comes from Greek and means "done by hand." The practice originated in the late 1890s with Daniel David Palmer, a self-taught healer in Iowa. He sought a cure for illness and disease that did not rely on drugs or surgery. Palmer reported curing deafness in a man who had lost his hearing after straining doing heavy work. Palmer attributed the hearing loss to a displaced vertebra and treated it by adjusting the man's spine.

Based on this and other cases he treated with spinal adjustments, Palmer advanced his theory that most disease is caused by misaligned vertebrae that impinge on spinal nerves. According to Palmer, correcting these misalignments reestablishes normal nerve and brain function, allowing the body to heal itself.

Through advancements in research and a deeper understanding of how the body works, the "bone out of place causing disease" theory has been debunked. However, what we have learnt is that when the spine is not moving correctly (the causes of which can be physical, chemical or emotional, as we will discuss further in the book), the brain then receives a distorted image of what the body is doing and how it is functioning.

This then results in a state of miscommunication, misinterpretation and maladaptation, placing the body into a state of "stress" and dysfunction.

The most common symptom that you will experience when this happens is stiffness and PAIN.

It has been shown that through specific, targeted and repeated adjustments of the spine, the brain and body become better "connected" resulting in an optimised state of function and maximised potential. This has been shown to vastly improve the quality of life and reduce the symptoms so many patients present with.

Many chiropractors focus on musculoskeletal problems of the spine, that is, conditions affecting the backbone and associated muscles. Chiropractors most commonly adjust the spine by using their hands to apply quick pressure on areas that are out of alignment or that do not have normal range of motion. Chiropractors also use mobilisation (manual therapy that does not involve a high-velocity thrust) as well as other techniques using specialized tools and soft-tissue work.

Chiropractic care is the most commonly used form of complementary and alternative medicine. Chiropractors are the third largest group of healthcare providers, after physicians and dentists, who treat patients directly. The American Medical Association (AMA) policy now states that it is ethical for physicians not only to associate professionally with chiropractors but also to refer patients to them for diagnostic or therapeutic services.

Family practitioners were the most likely physicians to refer to chiropractors, followed by family nurse practitioners, internists, neurologists, neurosurgeons, gynaecologists, and general surgeons. Chiropractors also frequently refer patients to other healthcare providers.[24]

Chiropractors are able to treat and manage:

- Ankle sprain (short term management)

- Cramps

- Elbow pain and tennis elbow (lateral epicondylitis) arising from associated musculoskeletal conditions of the back and neck, but not isolated occurrences

- Headache arising from the neck (cervicogenic)

- Joint pains

- Joint pains including hip and knee pain from osteoarthritis as an adjunct to core OA treatments and exercise

- General, acute and chronic backache, back pain (not arising from injury or accident)

- Generalised aches and pains

- Lumbago

- Mechanical neck pain (as opposed to neck pain following injury i.e. whiplash)

- Migraine prevention

- Minor sports injuries

- Muscle spasms

- Plantar fasciitis (short term management)

- Rotator cuff injuries, disease or disorders

- Sciatica

- Shoulder complaints (dysfunction, disorders and pain)

- Soft tissue disorders of the shoulder

- Tension and inability to relax

Regulated by the General Chiropractic Council (GCC) in the UK, (it is illegal to call yourself a chiropractor without being registered with this governing body) the profession is growing rapidly, with more and more seeking out chiropractic care to reduce pain and maximise the potential in their lives.

OSTEOPATHY

Osteopathy is a system of diagnosis and treatment for a wide range of medical conditions. It works with the structure and function of the body and is based on the principle that the well-being of an individual depends on the skeleton, muscles, ligaments and connective tissues functioning smoothly together.

To an osteopath, for your body to work well, its structure must also work well. So osteopaths work to restore your body to a state of balance, where possible, without the use of drugs or surgery. Osteopaths use touch, physical manipulation, stretching and massage to increase the mobility of joints, to relieve muscle tension, to enhance the blood and nerve supply to tissues, and to help your body's own healing mechanisms. They may also provide advice on posture and exercise to aid recovery, promote health and prevent symptoms recurring.

The American Osteopathic Association (AOA) states that the four major principles of osteopathic medicine are the following:

- The body is an integrated unit of mind, body, and spirit.

- The body possesses self-regulatory mechanisms, having the inherent capacity to defend, repair, and remodel itself.

- Structure and function are reciprocally interrelated.

- Rational therapy is based on consideration of the first three principles.

These principles are not held by Osteopaths to be empirical laws; they serve, rather, as the underpinnings of the osteopathic approach to health and disease.

Osteopaths are able to treat a large number of conditions:

- Arthritic pain

- Circulatory problems

- Cramp

- Digestion problems

- Fibromyalgia

- Frozen shoulder/ shoulder and elbow pain/ tennis elbow (lateral epicondylitis) arising from associated musculoskeletal conditions of the back and neck, but not isolated occurrences

- Headache arising from the neck (cervicogenic)

- Joint pains

- Joint pains including hip and knee pain from osteoarthritis as an adjunct to core OA treatments and exercise

- General, acute & chronic backache, back pain (not arising from injury or accident)

- Generalised aches and pains

- Lumbago

- Migraine prevention

- Minor sports injuries

- Muscle spasms

- Neuralgia

- Tension and inability to relax

- Rheumatic pain

- Sciatica

- Uncomplicated mechanical neck pain (as opposed to neck pain following injury i.e. whiplash)

At Banchory Spinal Health, we have found that chiropractors and osteopaths work very similarly towards a common goal, this is why we are proud to have both professions within our centre. This combined approach means all of our practitioners learn from each other and has shown to give amazing results over and over again.

MASSAGE THERAPY

Massage therapy is used at Banchory Spinal Health to help manage a health condition (alongside our Chiropractors and Osteopaths) or enhance relaxation and overall wellbeing.

It involves using hands or forearms to knead, stretch and manipulate the soft tissues of the body. Massage has been practiced in most cultures, both Eastern and Western, throughout human history, and was one of the earliest tools that people used to try to relieve pain.

The term "massage therapy" includes many techniques. The most common form of massage therapy in Western countries is called Swedish or classical massage; it is the core of most massage training programs.

Most massage therapists begin their careers with this training and then go on to learn other more advanced techniques, most commonly sports massage to accomplish specific goals such as releasing muscle spasms, working with specific pain conditions and advising on home exercises and treatment plans.

What can Massage Therapy Help With?

Massage therapy has been studied for several types of pain, including low-back pain, neck and shoulder pain, pain from osteoarthritis of the knee, and headaches. Studies are ongoing into how massage might positively influence psychological and mental wellbeing, and even how it will help premature infants to gain more weight!

The effects of massage are difficult to quantify from a research perspective, but from the results we see in clinic (and the popularity of massage alongside our other practitioner services) are enough for us to be certain that massage therapy is an essential service!

Although Massage Therapists tend not to "treat" specific conditions; we see our massage therapists as one of the key members of your healthcare team.

Exercise

"Motion is Lotion!"

KERRY WILSON

"To wild animals, movement is not a chore, not a temporary punishment for being physically lazy and out of shape, not an optional activity just for better looks."

ERWAN LE CORRE

MODERN MAN MOVEMENT VERSUS PRE-INDUSTRIAL MAN MOVEMENT

Before the Industrial Revolution, strenuous physical activity was a normal part in the daily lives of our ancestors. They worked hard to gather food and to provide shelter and safety to the community. But their physical exertion was not limited to the requirements of their work life. In those days, people engaged in 1- or 2-day periods of intense and strenuous exertion, followed by 1- or 2-day periods of rest and celebration.

However, even during these "rest" days, they made 6- to 20-mile round-trip visits to other villages to see relatives and friends and to trade with other clans or communities. They also took part in dancing and other social activities.[25]

Today, our physical activity is much lower than our pre-industrial age ancestors. Thanks to modern technology, we have very low levels of physical activity and high levels of sedentary behaviour. According to WHO estimates, about one in five adults were not active enough in 2010 globally (20% of men and 27% of women).[26]

"In less than two generations, physical activity has dropped by 20% in the UK and 32% in the U.S. In China, the drop is 45% in less than one generation. Vehicles, machines and technology now do our moving for us. What we do in our leisure time doesn't come close to making up for what we've lost."[27]

The biggest challenge that prevents us from walking or doing other kinds of physical activity is lack of time. Regular aerobic physical activity has to compete with the demands of home, work, school and community. It is my view that exercise needs to be a priority in our lives, and other commitments should work around it. Our enjoyment of life will be thoroughly depleted if we don't create or maintain an active body.

WE ARE DESIGNED TO MOVE

The human body works best when it's regularly active. From an evolutionary perspective, we were designed to move – to move about and engage in all manner of manual labour and activities throughout the day. This was essential to our survival as a species. The recent shift from a physically demanding life to a very sedentary one has been relatively sudden.

Moreover, during the past 20 years, the time we spend in front of screens (smartphones, computers, television and video games) and driving has increased dramatically. The health consequences of a sedentary life cannot be completely reversed by exercise. Therefore, we have to reduce our total sitting time in addition to regular moderate-to-intense exercise

Parents often tell their children to go out and play. Do adults need similar advice from their healthcare providers?[28]

THE RISKS OF SITTING

"Sitting is the new smoking." **DR. JAMES LEVINE**

Sitting too long has also been linked to a higher risk of earlier death.[29] Sitting for extended periods leads to contracture of the hip flexor and hamstring muscles, which negatively affects the lower back. Using a standing desk for a while can help to maintain better spinal alignment and muscle symmetry. However, standing still all day is also not ideal. Taking frequent breaks is the only way to ensure you're standing or sitting optimally. Also, take care of your posture: the top of the computer screen should be about eye level.

Breaking up sitting with standing or short walks relieves pain and fatigue and improves control of blood sugar, blood pressure and weight gain. I will often explain to our patients that they need to set a timer to go off every 30 minutes without fail, and when they hear the beep they have to get up and walk around the room/office for at least 1 minute. If everyone who worked at a computer did this, I believe we would see far fewer employee sick days due to back pain!

TYPES OF EXERCISE AND THEIR BENEFITS

"If you only have time to exercise or meditate but not both, then make exercise your daily meditation." **STEVE PAVLINA**

Strengthening, stretching, balance, and aerobic exercises are the four most important types of exercise, which will keep you active, mobile, and feeling great.

1. **Aerobic exercise**

   Aerobic exercise speeds up your heart rate and breathing and increases endurance. Aim for 150 minutes per week of moderate-intensity activity such as brisk walking, swimming, jogging, cycling, dancing, or classes like step aerobics.

2. **Strength training**

   As we age, we lose muscle mass. Strength training builds it back. Several studies show how even people in their nineties can increase their muscle mass by over 50%![30] Strengthening your muscles not only makes you stronger, but also reduces bone density loss (this is even more important in perimenopausal women), lowers blood sugar, helps weight control, improves balance and posture, and reduces stress and pain in the lower back and joints. Strength training includes bodyweight exercises like squats, push-ups, and lunges, and exercises against resistance from a weight, a band, or a weight machine.

3. **Stretching**

   Ageing leads to a loss of flexibility in the muscles and tendons. Stretching helps to improve flexibility, increases your range of motion, and reduces pain and the risk for injury. You need to stretch all parts of your body every day. Warm up your muscles first, and then perform static stretches for up to 60 seconds of the calves, thighs, lower back, shoulders, arms, and neck. Yoga is a perfect way to stretch regularly in a safe and mindful way.

4. **Balance exercises**

   Improving your balance helps prevent falls, which is extremely important as we get older. Balance exercises include standing on one foot (I often recommend this whilst washing dishes or brushing teeth) or walking heel to toe, with your eyes open or closed, and walking on uneven surfaces (trip to the beach anyone?). Yoga or tai chi classes are also excellent options to improve balance.[31]

Most people tend to focus on one activity or type of exercise and think they're doing enough. However, each type of exercise is different. Doing them all will give you more benefits. Mixing it up also helps to reduce boredom and cut your risk of injury. Also, some activities fit into more than one category. For example, many endurance activities also build strength. And some strength exercises can also help improve balance and flexibility.[32]

Yoga

Yoga is a mind and body practice that combines physical postures, breathing exercises, and relaxation. Yoga develops flexibility, endurance, balance, and muscle strength. Practising yoga has been shown to increase mindfulness not just in class but also in other areas of a person's life. Yoga is now being included in many cardiac rehabilitation programs due to its cardiovascular and stress-relieving benefits.

There are many types of yoga. Hatha yoga (a combination of many styles) is one of the most popular types. Hatha yoga focuses on pranayamas (breath-controlled exercises), asanas (yoga postures), and savasana (a resting period).[33]

Pilates

Pilates is named after its creator, Joseph Pilates, who developed the exercises in the 1920s. Pilates is a method of exercise that consists of low-impact flexibility, muscular strength and endurance movements. Pilates emphasizes proper postural alignment, core strength and muscle balance.

Many Pilates exercises can be done on the floor with just a mat.

The health benefits of Pilates include:

- Improved core strength and stability

- Improved posture and balance

- Improved flexibility

- Prevention and treatment of back pain

However, Pilates doesn't include aerobic exercise so you will need to complement it with aerobic exercises such as brisk walking, running, biking or swimming.[34]

Swimming

Swimming is great exercise because you have to move your whole body against the resistance of the water. Swimming is a good all-round activity because it:

- builds endurance, muscle strength and cardiovascular fitness

- tones muscles and builds strength

- helps maintain a healthy weight, heart and lungs

- provides a full-body workout, as almost all your body muscles are used during swimming.[35]

However, the swimming pool can be used not only for swimming but also for water aerobic exercises such as water walking, running, or jogging and vigorous aerobic exercises. Heated pools can help to warm up your joints and muscles. And aquatic exercise can improve physical functioning in adults over 50.[36]

Running

Studies have shown that running can help prevent obesity, type 2 diabetes, heart disease, high blood pressure, stroke, some cancers, and many other disorders. The health benefits of running include:

- It helps you live longer

- It helps you lose or maintain weight

- It improves the quality of your emotional and mental life

- It reduces your risk of cancer.[37]

Even 5 to 10 minutes a day of low-intensity running is enough to extend life by several years, compared with not running at all.[38] And the sweet spot for maximum longevity is up to 2.5 hours of running a week.[39]

Strength training

Strength training should be an important part of every fitness program. It helps you to reduce body fat, increase lean muscle mass and burn calories more efficiently. Strength training also helps you to:

- Develop/maintain strong bones

- Reduce or maintain your weight

- Enhance your quality of life

- Reduce the signs and symptoms of many chronic conditions, such as arthritis, back pain, obesity, heart disease, depression and diabetes.

- Sharpen your thinking and learning skills and improve your memory.

Strength training can be done at home or in the gym using:

- Bodyweight exercises such as push-ups, pull-ups, planks, lunges and squats.

- Free weights such as barbells and dumbbells.

- Resistance tubing, which is a lightweight tubing that provides resistance when stretched.

- Exercise machines[40]

Crossfit

CrossFit is a training program that builds strength and conditioning through extremely varied and challenging workouts. In CrossFit, everyone has to do the same workout each day.

Most CrossFit gyms will split their classes into three or four sections:

- Dynamic warm-up. It consists of jumps, jumping jacks, jump rope, squats, push-ups, lunges, pull-ups, functional movements, stretches, and mobility work.

- Skill or Strength work. If it's a strength day, you'll work on a pure strength movement like squats or deadlifts. If it's not a strength day, you'll work on a skill like one-legged squats.

- Workout of the day. You will either do a certain number of reps of particular exercises as quickly as possible or have a set time limit to do as many of a certain exercise as possible.

- Cool down and stretch. You're allowed to stretch out on your own or as a group.

A word of caution: CrossFit is not for everyone. If you have a history of injuries or medical conditions, it may not be the best choice for you. Most CrossFit gyms will let you attend one class for free. If you have a few in your area, try out each of them once before choosing the one that suits you best.[41]

Zumba/Jazzercise

Zumba and Jazzercise are fitness programs combining international music with dance moves. Zumba can be moderate or vigorous aerobic activity, depending on the intensity. They incorporate interval training (alternate fast and slow rhythms) and resistance training. The classes give you a powerful cardio workout while also building your coordination and agility. It's a full-body workout that is adaptable for any fitness level. The music, energetic environment, group experience and changing routines will have you sweating but in a fun way.[42]

Core Exercises

You use your core muscles to do everyday activities like tying your shoes and lifting heavy objects. It also affects your balance, posture, and stability.

The core includes your abdominal muscles as well as the muscles in your back and around your pelvis. Strengthening these muscles helps to stabilize your body, support your spine, and enhance your overall fitness. If you have a past or current back injury, speak to your practitioner about which core exercises might work well for you. They can show you how to safely tone and train your core.[43] Core exercises for beginners include the plank, crunches, bicycle crunch, leg raises, push-ups, and boat.[44]

WHEN SHOULD YOU EXERCISE?

The best time for exercise is different for each person. Work out at the time that is most suitable for you. The key is to do what's most likely to work for you because consistency is more important than timing.

For example, you might have heard that the best time to exercise is early in the morning. But if you're not a morning person, you may find it difficult to get up early to work out. Similarly, if you find that working out late in the evening stops you from falling asleep easily, you may have to exercise earlier in the day or try less intense forms of movement. Finally, if your schedule isn't predictable or you are travelling, you may need to be flexible and exercise whenever possible. What I love about the way the world is now is that exercise sequences can be accessed from anywhere in the world via YouTube. You can find a suitable programme for any level, with any amount of equipment required, at the touch of a button! Making the no-time-for-exercise excuse more difficult to float!

There's no one right time of day to exercise. So do it at the time that's best for you.[45]

DOES EXERCISE HAVE TO CHANGE WITH AGE?

We tend to underestimate and undermine the physical potential of our older generation. They can definitely exercise, even if they have diminished flexibility and functional capacity due to age and sedentary lifestyle. My advice will always be to consult your doctor before starting any exercise programme.

Motivation: Some of our more senior citizens might be nervous in an exercise setting, which may make them reluctant to try something new or different. However, most of them understand the dangers of inactivity and the benefits of exercise. Their exercise program should be individualised so that they feel confident and secure. Our society needs to normalize regular physical exercise and activities for *all ages*.

Safety: Safety is the most important concern with exercise programs for the elderly. They should exercise in well-lighted areas with user-friendly equipment. It is important that they work with a physical training professional who can make sure they are getting into exercise safely, if not just for the beginning of their exercise programme.

Set Realistic Goals: Before starting an exercise program, it is important to set individualised, realistic, and attainable goals. They should start with low to moderate level activity. The overall goal should be to improve strength, flexibility, body composition and cardiovascular endurance.

Warm-up and Flexibility: Each session should be started with a warm-up session such as walking and stretching all the joints for at least 10minutes. Similarly, the session should be ended with a cool-down period, which includes stretching and relaxation.

Aerobic Exercise: Aerobic activities such as walking, swimming, aqua exercise and cycling are all suitable for the older population. Swimming and aqua exercise cause less stress on the joints. Similarly, stationary cycling places less stress on the joints, while recumbent cycling puts less stress on the back. Walking at a higher pace than normal walking can be easily done in most environments and requires no additional equipment.

Strength Training: Muscular strength, functional mobility and balance can be significantly improved with resistance training under supervision. Everyone should do a resistance exercise program three days per week. They should be reminded to breathe regularly and not to hold their breath during resistance exercises.

A sedentary lifestyle leads to disability, early death, and a low quality of life. Chronological age does not represent quality of health. A range of opportunities for lifetime fitness is available for all ages. Preventing the complications associated with inactivity is far more cost-effective than the costs of long-term care.[46]

BEST RECOMMENDATIONS

"If we had a pill that contained all of the benefits of exercise, it would be the most widely prescribed drug in the world."
DR. RONALD DAVIS

- Move more and sit less to offset the risk of heart disease, high blood pressure, and mortality due to increased sedentary behaviour. Set a timer and stretch or take a short walk every 30-45 minutes.

- Move more frequently throughout the day. Integrate more movement into your daily life. Take the stairs instead of the lift. Walk short distances. Exercise while watching TV. Walk while talking on your mobile phone. Take every opportunity to move whenever and wherever you can!

OPTIMISE YOUR HEALTH

For the best health benefits from physical activity, you need at least 150 to 300 minutes of moderate-intensity aerobic activity like brisk walking or fast dancing each week. You also need to do muscle-strengthening exercises like push-ups or lifting weights, at least 2 days each week.[47]

Aerobic exercise and strength training are both important for improving your endurance and muscle mass. You also need to improve your flexibility and balance. Finding the right balance will depend on your individual goals, how quickly you want to achieve them, and the amount of time you can commit to exercising.[48]

I hope I have managed to impress upon you the importance of exercising regularly. I believe that we would see far fewer health issues if everyone prioritised exercise into their lives, and I want to do what I can to spread the message!

Attitude

"The greatest revolution of our generation is the discovery that human beings, by changing the inner attitudes of their minds, can change the outer aspects of their lives."

WILLIAM JAMES

"A healthy attitude is contagious but don't wait to catch it from others. Be a carrier."

TOM STOPPARD

A UK-wide stress survey was commissioned by the Mental Health Foundation between 29th March and 20th April 2018. A total of 4619 adults were surveyed online. The results are representative of all UK adults (aged 18+). The study is believed to be the largest and most comprehensive stress survey in the UK.

The highlights of the report:

- **74% of UK adults felt so stressed at some point over the last year that they felt overwhelmed or unable to cope.**

- **32% of adults said they had experienced suicidal feelings as a result of stress.**

- **16% of adults said they had self-harmed as a result of stress.**

The study is included in a new report by the Mental Health Foundation.

After the survey, Mental Health Foundation Director, Isabella Goldie said:

> *"Millions of us around the UK are experiencing high levels of stress and it is damageing our health. Stress is one of the great public health challenges of our time, but it still isn't being taken as seriously as physical health concerns.*
>
> *"Stress is a significant factor in mental health problems including anxiety and depression. It is also linked to physical health problems like heart disease, problems with our immune system, insomnia and digestive problems. Individually we need to understand what is causing us personal stress and learn what steps we can take to reduce it for ourselves and those around us.[49]*

So it's hardly new information that we are far more stressed than we should be. However, what many people might not realise is the physical influence that these stress levels have on our body. I fully believe that most physical illnesses are a result (on some level) of our emotional stresses. This next section covers how stress can change our physiology and what effects that might have.

DOES MY ATTITUDE INFLUENCE MY PAIN?

"Pain is inevitable; suffering is not." **THE BUDDHA**

Pain is defined as "an unpleasant sensory and emotional experience associated with actual or potential tissue damage, or described in terms of such damage". Pain is a sensation of the body but is almost always an unpleasant emotional experience too.

Pain is the leading reason for patients seeking medical care and is one of the most disabling, burdensome, and costly conditions. It could be said that pain is the true pandemic in our lives! 8.9 million estimated working days were lost due to musculoskeletal disorders in 2019/20, with each person taking 18.4 days off over the 12 month period.[50]

The following factors can affect our perception of and reaction to pain:

1. our existing beliefs about pain

2. our beliefs about our ability to control pain

3. earlier experiences of pain

4. expectations of recovery

5. current emotional states (including catastrophising, anxiety, and depression)[51]

HOW DOES MY MENTAL STATE AFFECT PAIN?

There is no shortage of studies to confirm that negative emotions can cause physical pain[52] and recent research has now confirmed that the neural pathways (the parts of your brain that "light up") when you experience emotional pain, overlap with the pathways that are involved with physical pain.[53]

To put it simply, when we are stressed, a sequence of events is triggered in our brain (called the hypothalamic-pituitary-adrenal axis) which cause our adrenal glands (located just above your kidneys!) to release hormones called glucocorticoids. The most well-known glucocorticoid is called cortisol. This is known as the "stress hormone".

Cortisol is essential for many processes in the body, and it can be very helpful in times when we are in acute danger and need to make a quick get-away or fight a sabre tooth tiger (so mostly back in the cavemen days!). However, what we see more and more is that many of our patients suffer with a lower grade level of stress all the time. This causes their cortisol levels to become raised consistently, which is not really what cortisol is meant to do.

Cortisol is responsible for:

- Increasing blood pressure by narrowing arteries and heart beating faster

- Taking blood from your organs and pumping it into your extremities

- Increasing blood sugar levels

- Moving fat cells to abdomen (yes you read that right – stress can make you fat around your tummy!)

- Hormonal concerns such as erectile dysfunction and menstrual changes

- Promoting inflammation in your body

Studies have shown that when you have increased levels of cortisol in your body, you are more likely to experience higher levels of pain.[54] They also go on to show that the more a person negatively thinks about certain events, the more likely they are to secrete higher levels of cortisol. So it would appear that a negative cycle is happening – the more we worry about our pain levels, the more cortisol heightens our pain and increases the inflammation in our bodies!

This is why one of the main things we tell patients when they start their care plans with us is that they should STOP WORRYING about their pain, as that will only make it worse. Plus, stress can cause so many other health issues, I really would encourage everyone to take the necessary steps to reduce their stress.

MIND-BODY CONNECTION

"The brain and peripheral nervous system, the endocrine and immune systems, and indeed, all the organs of our body and all the emotional responses we have, share a common chemical language and are constantly communicating with one another." **DR JAMES GORDON (FOUNDER OF THE CENTER FOR MIND-BODY MEDICINE)**

The mind-body connection means that our thoughts, feelings, beliefs, and attitudes can affect the functioning of our body positively or negatively. On the other hand, what we eat, how much we exercise, and even our posture can affect our mental state, either positively or negatively. This results in a constant, complex interaction between our "minds" and "bodies".

Mind-body therapies use the body to influence the mind and vice versa. These include

- Meditation

- Prayer

- Yoga

- Tai chi

- Qigong

- Biofeedback

- Relaxation

- Hypnosis

- Guided imagery

- Cognitive behavioural therapy

- Creative arts therapies (art, music, or dance)

It's important to note that the mind is not the same as the brain.

- The mind consists of mental states such as thoughts, emotions, beliefs, attitudes, and images. (think of it as software)

- The brain is the organ that allows us to experience these mental states. (think of it as hardware)

Mental states can be conscious or unconscious. Each mental state causes a positive or negative effect in the physical body. For example, the mental state of anxiety causes the production of **stress hormones**. Many mind body therapies help you to become more conscious of your mental and emotional states. You can then use this awareness to guide your thoughts and emotions in a better and more positive direction.[55]

WHAT IS A HEALTHY MIND?

"The key to a healthy life is having a healthy mind." **RICHARD DAVIDSON**

A healthy mind is not merely the absence of mental disease. According to the World Health Organization (WHO), mental health is "a state of well being in which the individual realizes his or her own abilities, can cope with the normal stresses of life, can work productively and fruitfully, and is able to make a contribution to his or her community."[56]

There are some really simple and feasible ways in which you can positively affect your mental health and emotional wellbeing:

- **Be active**
  Movement and exercise boost your mood. They also help you to sleep better and get the rest you need.

- **Lower your alcohol intake**
  Alcohol can increase feelings of depression and also affect your physical health.

- **Connect with family and friends**
  Quality time with your loved ones is the best way to boost your mental wellbeing.

- **Reduce your sugar intake**
  When you eat a large amount of sugar you will feel a temporary sugar "high". However, you will also notice a hefty dip afterwards, which in some people can contribute to negative thoughts and depression.

- **Try new things**
  Learn a new sport, language, learn to play an instrument, read books and feed your mind with positive inspiration and variety.[57]

ATTITUDE OF GRATITUDE

Changing your default *attitude* to one of *gratitude* could be the most important thing that you learn from this book. The benefits of practicing gratitude on a regular basis are endless! People who regularly practice gratitude by taking time to notice and reflect upon the things they're thankful for experience more positive emotions, feel more alive, sleep better, express more compassion and kindness, have stronger social relationships, have better self-esteem and even have stronger immune systems.[58]

Practicing gratitude doesn't necessarily mean you have to make any large over the top gestures of thanks to others. Research by psychologist Robert Emmons, showed that simply keeping a gratitude journal – regularly writing brief reflections on moments for which we're thankful – can significantly increase wellbeing and life satisfaction.

Of course, we all start these practices with the greatest intentions, however for most of us this motivation lasts about three days until writing in my gratitude journal every evening soon gets forgotten about in lieu of a good book or thriller on Netflix.

I have discovered that there are some really simple ways to practice gratitude on a really manageable scale.

Be Specific

The best way to really feel grateful for the little things is to notice new things you're grateful for, every day. The things you might be grateful for will have more emotional impact (and therefore more likely to imprint long-term on your brain) if they are exact and specific to what has happened that day. For example, I might be grateful for: "My husband cooking dinner so I could have a bath as I had had a difficult day" instead of just "my husband". Or I am grateful for "having the ability to get a lovely coffee made for me at Starbucks" as opposed to "coffee". This can take some getting used to but after a while it becomes a fun game.

Don't Keep it to Yourself

One of the biggest determinants (if not the biggest) of happiness is the quality of our relationships with others. Therefore, it might make sense to think of other people as we develop our gratitude practice. Robert Emmons recommends that focusing our gratitude on people rather than circumstances or material items will boost the benefits we experience. You could even extend this idea by including others in your gratitude practice. You could write a thank-you letter to someone who had an impact on you or share your grateful thought of the day around the dinner table with your family. If you have children, this might help develop their gratitude mindset from an early age!

Feel the Gratitude!

Although research suggests that writing in a gratitude journal will have the greatest positive effect on your attitude, if that doesn't feel doable for you then just taking 3 minutes out of your day to *feel* that for which you are grateful, might be almost as effective. When I feel pushed for time and I have forgotten to write in my gratitude journal, I will take some time to tell myself what I am grateful for and amplify the experience of it in my mind. A great example of this: Recently I had a very challenging day. I did not have a lot of time so I took 3 minutes to sit down and thought of something simple and specific I was grateful for. In this instance I thought of my bed. We have a super king size bed which can fit the whole family in it when needed! I pictured lying in my big comfy bed, under my snuggly duvet and thanked the bed for taking such good care of me and my family and told myself I was grateful to have such a large bed for us to sleep in safely. Immediately I felt a weight lift from my shoulders and this quick and easy exercise re-framed the rest of my day.

SLEEP

"A good laugh and a long sleep are the two best cures for anything." **IRISH PROVERB**

For me, the importance of a good night's sleep is up there with exercise and a healthy diet. Research has shown that if you experience poor sleep, here will be an immediate negative effect on your hormones, exercise performance, and brain function.[59] It can also cause weight gain and increase disease risk in both adults and children.[60 61 62]

Already we can see how much a healthy sleep pattern may positively affect your physical and mental health.

There are a number of evidence-based tips I can offer to help you get a better night's sleep:

1. Increase exposure to sunlight or bright light during the day

2. Reduce exposure to light (particularly blue light from screens) in the evening

3. Limit or stop caffeine consumption, particularly after midday

4. Reduce daytime naps unless they are under 30mins (or you are a baby!)

5. Try to sleep and wake at consistent times

6. Limit or stop alcohol consumption

7. Make sure your bedroom is quiet, calm and relaxing

8. Don't eat after 8pm, stop eating earlier if possible

9. Integrate relaxation or meditation techniques before bed

10. Take a bath or shower before bed

11. Exercise regularly but not before bed!

12. Limit or stop any liquid consumption before bed

Sleep Position

This is one of the most commonly asked questions at Banchory Spinal Health. There are a few top tips we like to give when people ask about sleeping positions:

DO NOT sleep on your front. This is like me telling you to turn your head 90degrees to one side, then asking you to stay like that for 8 hours. Your neck and the rest of your spine will not be happy about that.

Lying on your back (prone) is optimal, however, do not do this if you have been diagnosed with sleep apnoea.

Side lying is perfectly good. However, depending on the width of your shoulders you might benefit from a rolled-up towel in your pillowcase, along the bottom of the pillow where your neck would be. Ask your practitioner to demonstrate this!

Some people find that tucking another pillow in between your knees when side lying helps to reduce any torsion in their pelvis if they have suffered with lower back/pelvic problems.

NEVER use more than one pillow (unless your life depends on it if you're a sleep apnoea sufferer!) as this will force your neck into forward flexion which puts unnecessary pressure on your neck joints and muscles.

Should I have a soft or firm mattress?

Many people have tried and failed to determine through research what kind of mattress is optimal for healthy sleep. My advice is to try before you buy. I personally love a firm mattress, and my spine likes it too! That being said, I know many who love a softer mattress or memory foam and they find that better for their backs. Take advantage of the shops and companies that are willing to let you in store to lie on them, or will send you mattresses to try at home.

Some people find it much easier to sleep, and get a better quality of sleep when they take 10 minutes to relax their mind before getting into bed.

MINDFUL MEDITATION

Meditation involves focussing the mind to increase awareness of the present moment. This method helps us cope with pain and stress and can be easily done anywhere. An example of mindful meditation would be to sit up straight, close your eyes, and focus your attention on your incoming and outgoing breathing. This exercise could be done for just a couple of minutes or longer. It helps you to let your thoughts come and go while being aware of your respiration. It can be most helpful during stressful times and difficult life events, but really we should all be taking time out to do this every day.

Mindful meditation can create a sense of control, which helps you to make your experience of pain more manageable. Yoga, tai chi and other mind-body techniques are also recommended to get the same benefits.[63]

My favourite meditation resources are:

- Calm™ and Headspace™ both apps for your phone

- Youtube is a great source of free guided meditations and mindfulness sessions

I used to think meditation was only for certain types of people, but I now class it as a basic essential for a healthy life. If you take only one action from reading this book, please let it be introducing a daily meditation practice.

LOVE AND HEALTH

"The best and most beautiful things in this world cannot be seen or even heard, but must be felt with the heart." **HELEN KELLER**

"Far too many people are looking for the right person, instead of trying to be the right person." **GLORIA STEINEM**

According to a growing body of scientific research, love gives you exceptional health benefits. Dr Helen Riess, director of the Empathy and Relational Science Program at Massachusetts General Hospital, lists these five health benefits of love:

1. **Love makes you happy.**
   When you first fall in love, dopamine, the feel-good brain chemical associated with reward, is activated. It makes you feel positive and appreciated and this naturally is good for your health.

2. **Love busts stress.**
   After the initial phase, another brain chemical, oxytocin or the bonding hormone is activated. It reduces stress levels and creates greater homeostasis and balance.

3. **Love eases anxiety.**
   Being in love and feeling close to another person can reduce the anxiety about loneliness and insecurity.

4. **Love makes you take better care of yourself.**
   Couples encourage each other to go to the doctor when they don't want to. Sometimes, partners will even notice early signs of health problems before the sufferer.

5. **Love helps you live longer.**
   Research has shown that married couples enjoy greater longevity

than singles because of consistent social and emotional support and better adherence to medical care.[64] Also, a partner can hold you accountable to a healthy lifestyle and steer you away from unhealthy behaviour. Married couples have lower rates of substance abuse,[65] lower blood pressure and less depression[66] than singles.[67]

I know what you're thinking – what if you have not yet found that person to love? Not a problem! Many people find that having a furry companion is just as oxytocin-inducing as their human counterparts. In May 2013, the American Heart Association (AHA) released a scientific statement associating pet ownership (more so dogs) with reduced heart disease risk factors and greater life expectancy.[68] There are many theories as to why this might be, it could of course just be the case that healthier people are more likely to own dogs, however a dog provides you with unconditional love, companionship, and a reason for daily exercise! Don't have time for a dog? Many people borrow dogs or volunteer at animal shelters to get their animal fix – this will increase your health and also the health of your community!

Love Your Food

"A healthy outside starts from the inside."

ROBERT URICH

"The food you eat can be either the safest and most powerful form of medicine or the slowest form of poison."

ANN WIGMORE

The proverbial saying 'You are what you eat' means that you need to eat good food to be fit and healthy. It's literally true! The structure and function of every cell in your body depends on the nutrients you get from your food. You are constantly repairing and rebuilding yourself. A nutritious and healthy diet can help you build healthy cells.[69]

THE MINEFIELD OF NUTRITION

The world of nutrition is constantly evolving as new research gets churned out at a rapid pace. It is also true that a particular way of eating that works for one person might not be the best choice for others – we are all different!

I strongly believe in making healthy eating as easy and simple as possible, whilst still enjoying "treats" (after all, what is life without cake?). So, before I get into exactly *what* you should be eating, I would like to share my top tips for making healthy eating achievable for everyone.

1. Prepare and pack your lunch! Don't get caught out with nothing with you, resulting in purchasing quick and unhealthy food that is not good for your body.

2. Plan your meals for the week, so you purposefully buy good food you intend to eat and aren't tempted to throw in any extras!

3. If you don't have any naughty snacks in the house, then you won't eat them in the evenings! Treat yourselves on Saturdays but only buy enough "treat" for one day!

4. Be mindful of the nutritional value of your drinks. Water is always the best choice!

5. Try to eat as many different colours of foods as possible, this will help your gut microbiome flourish in a positive way!

6. Alcohol consumption every day is definitely not a good idea, it has no nutritional value.

7. If in doubt, eat more vegetables!

ANTI-INFLAMMATORY FOODS

Regularly we come across patients who are suffering from too much inflammation in their body. In our line of work this mostly manifests as pain, but can also manifest as skin conditions, digestive problems and even inflammatory arthritis. Inflammation in your body can happen from physical trauma (and emotional stress as we talked about earlier) and also chemical stress within your body. Many major diseases that plague us – including cancer, heart disease, diabetes, arthritis, depression, and Alzheimer's – have been linked to chronic inflammation.[70]

For that reason, I would think it sensible if you were suffering with chronic pain (and any other of the disease mentioned above) to introduce an anti-inflammatory way of eating alongside the manual therapies we provide. I would think this likely to produce better health outcomes.

As a rough guide, here are the foods that we know promote the inflammatory responses in your body:

- Sugar

- Refined carbohydrates such as white bread/pastry/pasta/cereals (your body converts these into sugar!)

- Fried foods

- Highly processed meat and grain-fed red meat

- Trans fats (often found in baked goods)

- Dairy products (not all dairy products are created equal, and this isn't true for everyone)

- Alcohol (although some studies show a limited amount of red wine actually has the opposite effect!)

SO WHAT SHOULD YOU BE EATING?

Vegetables should be the main thing you eat. Consider eating a salad or soup for lunchtimes. Remember to eat as many different colours as possible and a good mix of raw and lightly cooked vegetables is perfect

- Oily fish has been shown to help combat inflammation (salmon, tuna, sardines)

- Nuts are a great source of protein (not peanuts! And no roasted and salted nuts!)

- Beans and pulses are a wonderful budget friendly way of getting fibre and protein in your diet.

- Extra virgin olive oil (not heated!) is the perfect addition to your lunchtime salads!

- Fresh fruit is packed with antioxidants and fibre. Great to satisfy a sweet craving too!

To reduce levels of inflammation, aim for a *mostly* healthy diet. I like to eat well at least 80% of the time, which allows me some treats on weekends. This helps me to keep my balance and still enjoy life! If you're looking for an eating plan that closely follows the tenets of anti-inflammatory eating, consider the Mediterranean diet, which is high in fruits, vegetables, nuts, whole grains, fish, and healthy oils.

With all new eating plans, consider speaking to a dietician or nutritionist to help you plan your meals.

"Healthy eating is a way of life, so it's important to establish routines that are simple, realistic, and ultimately liveable." **HORACE**

BEST RECOMMENDATIONS

"Moderation. Small helpings. Sample a little bit of everything. These are the secrets of happiness and good health." **JULIA CHILD**

Your long-term health results are dependent on your behaviour, not necessarily just your diet. For a healthy body and healthy body weight, you have to develop consistent, sustainable daily habits. For example, instead of eating 800 calories one day and then eating 3,000 calories the next day, aim to eat just above the amount you can stick with, and reduce it in small amounts over time, if needed. Aim for consistent progress in small increments.

Time

HEALING TAKES TIME

Good health takes time and commitment. Your symptoms didn't develop overnight. They are usually a gradual but progressive build-up of physical changes.

However, we live in an age of instant gratification. Most of us tend to be impatient and want instant relief. It is far easier to pop a pill when we are in pain than to consider the longer-term lifestyle changes required to improve our situation. Unfortunately, instant relief is not healing. Instant relief masks our symptoms without restoring the body to its natural healthy state.

For example, most drugs give instant relief by stopping the brain from feeling our symptoms. So, you have to keep taking them to continue to get relief. However, when we discontinue the drug, the symptoms will likely return. Ideally, the drug should correct the problem so that we can stop taking the drug after a reasonable period. Usually, that is not the case.

For example, have you ever known anyone whose anti-diabetes medications healed them of diabetes so they could discontinue the drug? How about high blood pressure? Migraine? Heart disease? Usually, we have to take them for the rest of our lives, because medications can control the symptoms of these disorders but cannot reverse or cure them.

On the other hand, a nutritional and lifestyle program addresses the real root causes of your illness. If you stay on the program for the prescribed duration, you get better and regain your health.

Real healing takes time. It may take several months to fully recover from a chronic pain issue or health problem. It may even take several years to completely overcome a degenerative condition. However, it doesn't take that long to see improvement. Just as a seed sprouts and begins to grow long before the plant matures fully, you can see the signs that your health is improving long before you are completely healed.

Bear this in mind when considering how quickly you expect to feel better after having had back pain for the last 5 years!

WHAT IS A REASONABLE AMOUNT OF TIME FOR HEALING?

The time you take to heal depends on many factors such as the nature of the disorder, your immunity, your lifestyle, the severity and duration of the illness, your stress levels and many other things. With acute illness, you should see some improvement within a day or two. Chronic illnesses may take a few weeks or months to improve. Degenerative illnesses may take even longer, especially if they involve organs, bones and joints.

Improvement means you should feel better. The true test of any therapy is how it affects your body and mind. Do you feel more energetic? Is your sense of well-being improving? Are you feeling more alive and healthier? You need to learn to listen to your own body and trust what it is telling you.

The vast number of challenges our body can face, all have different responses, and every person's response is unique. What we do know, is that true healing and correction are not instantaneous (and if they were, they would be unsustainable); time is the KEY to making true change. Small, specific, sustained changes bring about the biggest and sustainable change – be patient with your body, it certainly is patient with you.

I have lost count of how often our patients say it is their age that results in them feeling and presenting the way that they are, but is this necessarily true and does age effect healing? Is age associated with longer healing times? Let's have a look.

AGE-RELATED LOSS OF FLEXIBILITY

In healthy older adults aged 55 to 85 years, age-related loss of flexibility appears to be small such that the normal loss of joint range of motion is unlikely to affect daily functions or cause disability.[71]

Many age-related changes including declines in flexibility are caused by disuse and a sedentary lifestyle. Men are more likely to have decreased flexibility than women.

Exercise, stretching, yoga, and regular manual therapies can reverse many age-related changes including decreased flexibility.

WHY DOES THE BODY AGE?

Ageing is a complex process that affects different people and even different organs in diverse ways. No single process can explain all the changes caused by ageing. It's due to the interaction of many lifelong influences, including environment, diet, exercise, past illnesses, genes, lifestyle, and many other factors.

The cause and mechanism of ageing are not clear. It could be a predetermined process controlled by genes or it could be due to long-term injuries, caused by ultraviolet light or the by-products of metabolism such as free radicals.

Each person ages differently. Although some changes always occur with ageing, they occur at different rates and to different extents. Some systems begin ageing as early as age 30. Other ageing processes are not common until much later in life. There is no way to predict exactly how you will age.[72] However, there is no need to feel depressed or anxious about ageing. Most of the significant age-related health issues can be minimised by a healthy lifestyle and a positive attitude. As Mark Twain said, "Age is an issue of mind over matter. If you don't mind, it doesn't matter." He also said, "Wrinkles should merely indicate where smiles have been."

A FINAL THOUGHT ON TIME

Time, movement, hydration, balanced nutrition, the correct therapeutic modalities and a positive mindset are all vital in healing; and all need to be addressed when proactively working towards health. If you have a health challenge, particularly a chronic one, think about how long it has taken for your body to get that way. Often it has been struggling for years. When embarking on a lifestyle change to improve your health, it will be a marathon, not a sprint. Be patient and concerted in your efforts, it really is that simple.

Hydrate

"You are 87% water; the other 13% keeps you from drowning."

P. E. MORRIS

"Drinking water is like washing out your insides. The water will cleanse the system, fill you up, decrease your caloric load and improve the function of all your tissues."

KEVIN R. STONE

Good hydration is vital for good health.

Water makes up about two thirds of your body and about 73% of your brain.[73] Every organ in your body needs water to function properly. You need water to maintain your body temperature, get rid of waste, lubricate your joints and for general good health.[74] Good hydration has been shown to reduce the risk of some health disorders such as constipation, hypertension, kidney stones, urinary tract infections and exercise-induced asthma.[75]

HOW MUCH WATER DO YOU NEED?

Water is essential for the maintenance of normal physical and cognitive functions and normal thermoregulation.[76] Based on the European Food Safety Authority's scientific estimation of adequate water intake, men should aim for a total water intake of 2.5 litres per day whereas women should aim for a total water intake of 2 litres per day. Ideally, 70-80% of this should come from drinks and 20-30% from foods.[77]

AVERAGE WATER INPUT = 2.5 LITRES	AVERAGE WATER OUTPUT = 2.5 LITRES
Water in fluids: 1.5 litres	Urine: 1.6 litres
Water in food: 0.7 litres	Sweat: 0.45 litres
Metabolic water: 0.3 litres	Breathing: 0.35 litres
	Faeces: 0.2 litres
Total: 2.5 litres	Total: 2.5 litres

Water balance in sedentary adults living in temperate climate[78]

Usually, the contribution of food to total dietary fluid intake is 20–30% whereas 70–80% is provided by drinks. This relationship is not fixed and depends on the type of drinks and the choice of foods. Foods have a wide range of water content (from less than 40% to more than 80%).

Your water requirement changes throughout the day. Ideally, your water intake should equal your water requirement over 24 hours.[79]

If water intake is less than our requirement, we become dehydrated. This is more likely in hot and dry conditions, especially if we have limited access to water and lose more water than usual through excessive sweating, diarrhoea or vomiting.

Our organs, joints and even the discs in our spine are made mostly of water. For this reason, we ALWAYS encourage our patients to increase their water consumption.

DIFFERENT FORMS OF FLUIDS

Water: Science has proved the truth of this ancient Slovakian proverb, "Pure water is the world's first and foremost medicine." Water has zero calories and is the best way to quench your thirst. Drink tap water. You don't need to drink bottled water; tap water is good enough. However, you may need to filter it before drinking. To make water more refreshing, add a slice of lemon or lime.

Tea and coffee: You should limit your daily caffeine intake to about 400 mg, which is equal to 750 ml of black coffee (3 cups) or 1 litre of black tea per day (4 cups). If you are pregnant, limit your caffeine intake to 500 ml of coffee (2 cups) or 750 ml of tea (3 cups). Drink herbal tea or decaffeinated coffee or tea if you want to have more than the recommended amount of caffeinated drinks. Avoid speciality coffees and teas because they are high in sugar.

Fruit and vegetable juice: Limit your intake of fruit juices since they are high in calories and low in fibre. Eat the fruit instead. Make sure you choose 100% real fruit juice. Avoid fruit drinks, cocktails or punches as they have added sugar and few nutrients.

Milk: If you enjoy drinking milk, aim for 500 ml of organic milk (2 cups) or its alternatives such as almond milk, oat milk, hemp milk, coconut milk, rice milk, cashew milk, or macadamia milk as part of your fluid intake for the day. These milk alternatives are especially useful if you have lactose/dairy intolerance.

Broth and soups: Broth and broth-based soups are a good source of fluid. However, most canned soups and broths have too much added salt and sugar. Choose soups low in salt/sugar or the best option would be to make your own.

Fizzy drinks: Avoid these drinks because they are high in calories, sugar and chemicals. Some fizzy drinks like colas may also contain caffeine. Diet fizzy drinks are calorie and sugar free but may have caffeine, artificial sweeteners and other chemicals.

Sports drinks: Commercial sports drinks are usually not needed to keep hydrated when you exercise. Many of them contain ingredients that are unhealthy. Water and a healthy diet can replace water and minerals lost during exercise.[80]

Alcohol: Minimize alcoholic drinks. The immediate effects of cutting down alcohol include feeling better in the morning, being less tired during the day, better-looking skin, feeling more energetic, and better weight management. Long-term benefits include improved mood, sleep, judgement, memory, immunity, behaviour, and overall health.[81] Of course the occasional alcoholic drink is fine!

DEHYDRATION IN THE UK

A survey carried out by the Royal National Lifeboat Institution showed that 89% of the population is not drinking enough water to maintain healthy hydration levels. Men are less hydrated than women: 20% of men drink no water at all during the day compared with 13% of women. The elderly are less hydrated: 25% of those over 55 stated that they drink no water during the day compared with 7% of those aged 25-34.[82]

TOP TIPS FOR HEALTHY HYDRATION

1. Drink water. It is the best way to hydrate as it has no calories, sugar or artificial chemicals. Heed these words of Thoreau, "Water is the only drink for a wise man."

2. Choose food with high water content such as soups, stews, vegetables, and fruits to increase your overall daily water intake.

3. Sip water regularly throughout the day because hydration levels fluctuate throughout the day.

4. Drink more water when you exercise or spend time in hot and dry environments.

5. Make sure to carry water with you, especially when you are travelling. Keep water nearby when you are at work, at school or playing.

6. Make sure you are drinking pure water. Use a water filter if necessary.

7. Avoid or minimize unhealthy drinks such as soft drinks, caffeinated drinks and alcohol.[83]

FINAL TIP – LISTEN TO YOUR BODY

- **Check your thirst:** If you are thirsty or have a dry mouth, you may not be drinking enough water. Remember that when you are thirsty, you are already somewhat dehydrated. Aim to drink fluids often throughout the day.

- **Check your urine:** If your urine is a dark yellow colour and has a strong smell, you may not be getting enough fluids. Urine that is light yellow or clear in colour usually means that you are drinking enough fluids. The amount of urine you make can also be a sign of your hydration status. If you do not make much urine throughout the day and it is dark in colour, you need more fluids.

- **Check your mood:** If you feel tired, are not able to focus or have headaches, these could be signs that you are dehydrated.[84]

Parting Words

"Health is the new wealth. We will still define success by how nice our house is or the zip code we live in. But going forward, health is going to become increasingly synonymous with social status. Health will be a currency of its own. You cannot necessarily buy health, but you will know how to earn it, and you earn it every day of your life."

HENRY LOUBET, CEO, BOHEMIA HEALTH

"Never doubt that a small group of thoughtful, committed citizens can change the world; indeed, it's the only thing that ever has."

MARGARET MEAD

Congratulations on finishing the book! Whether you read every page or read the chapters that were of interest to you, you took the first step. This is more than most people manage already!

Nine out of ten people who purchase books don't finish them. That's why *Groucho Marx* said, 'From the moment I picked up y our book until I put it down, I was convulsed with laughter. *Some day* I intend *reading it.*'

You are in the tiny minority of people who have decided to take charge of your health and seek information and help. That is the first right step.

As already explained, the vital principles that will help you to achieve your health goals are:

H – Hands on Health

E – Exercise

A – Attitude

L – Love your Food

T – Time

H – Hydrate

The most important takeaway from this book is that you have to take responsibility for your own health by nurturing your body and mind. And that starts with making the right choices, and just trying to do a little better than you did before.

The journey of a thousand miles begins with the first step. Choose one baby step that you can do right now. Go for a walk, or run. Or drink a glass of water. Or spend some quality time with your family. Whatever it is, do it right now.

One final caveat: Each one of us is different with individual health issues determined by our age, gender, genes, environment, emotions, and past illnesses. I have to tell you to consult your doctor before embarking on any major lifestyle changes, particularly if you are currently being medically managed for anything.

I hope this book was helpful to you. If you have any questions or comments, please find us at www.banchoryspinalhealth.co.uk. We would love to hear from you.

Wishing you all the best in these next steps of your happy, healthy life.

Felicity and the team at Banchory Spinal Health

"Happily ever after is not a fairy tale – it's a choice." **FAWN WEAVER**

REFERENCES

1   Fuster V, Kelly BB, editors. Promoting Cardiovascular Health in the Developing World: a critical challenge to achieve global health. Washington, D.C.: The National Academies Press, Institute of Medicine; 2010. https://www.ncbi.nlm.nih.gov/books/NBK45693/

2   https://www.who.int/news-room/fact-sheets/detail/the-top-10-causes-of-death

3   Fleming D, William H. Welch and the rise of modern medicine. Boston, Massachusetts: Little, Brown; 1954.

4   Mokdad AH, Marks JS, Stroup DF, Gerberding JL. Actual causes of death in the United States, 2000. JAMA. 2004;291:1238–45. https://www.ncbi.nlm.nih.gov/pubmed/15010446

5   https://jamanetwork.com/journals/jama/fullarticle/2778234

6   https://www.health.org.uk/news-and-comment/blogs/health-and-social-care-funding

7   https://www.ncbi.nlm.nih.gov/pmc/articles/PMC4339086/

8   http://articles.mercola.com/sites/articles/archive/2014/03/15/bad-american-health-care-system.aspx

9   https://www.england.nhs.uk/statistics/statistical-work-areas/ae-waiting-times-and-activity/ae-attendances-and-emergency-admissions-2019-20/

10   Cathy Schoen, Robin Osborn, Michelle M. Doty, Meghan Bishop, Jordon Peugh and Nandita Murukutla. Toward Higher-Performance Health Systems: Adults' Health Care Experiences In Seven Countries, 2007. Commonwealth Fund in New York City

11   https://www.finder.com/uk/health-statistics

12   https://www.ncbi.nlm.nih.gov/pubmed/17469345

13   https://www.rcoa.ac.uk/faculty-of-pain-medicine/opioids-aware

14   https://www.bmj.com/content/352/bmj.i20

15   https://www.thelancet.com/journals/lanpsy/article/PIIS2215-0366(18)30471-1/fulltext

16   https://www.thetimes.co.uk/article/britains-opioid-epidemic-kills-five-every-day-83md7wc3k

17   https://www.hhs.gov/surgeongeneral/priorities/opioids-and-addiction/index.
      html

18   https://www.finder.com/uk/health-statistics

19   https://www.actuaries.org.uk/news-and-insights/media-centre/media-
      releases-and-statements/longer-term-influences-driving-lower-life-expectancy-
      projections

20   https://www.forthwithlife.co.uk/blog/great-britain-and-stress/

21   Preamble to the Constitution of WHO as adopted by the International Health
      Conference, New York, 19 June – 22 July 1946; signed on 22 July 1946 by the
      representatives of 61 States (Official Records of WHO, no. 2, p. 100) and entered
      into force on 7 April 1948. The definition has not been amended since 1948.

22   The University of Arizona Center of Integrative Medicine. What is Integrative
      Medicine? https://integrativemedicine.arizona.edu/about/definition.html

23   https://insights.ovid.com/crossref?an=00005768-201803000-00015

24   Christensen MG, Kollasch MW, Hyland JK. Practice analysis of chiropractic,
      2010. A project report, survey analysis, and summary of the practice of
      chiropractic within the United States. Greeley, CO: National Board of
      Chiropractic Examiners; 2010

25   U.S. Department of Health and Human Services. Physical Activity and Health:
      A Report of the Surgeon General. Atlanta, GA: U.S. Department of Health and
      Human Services, Centers for Disease Control and Prevention, National Center
      for Chronic Disease Prevention and Health Promotion, 1996

26   https://www.who.int/news-room/fact-sheets/detail/physical-activity

27   https://www.icsspe.org/bookshop/designed-move

28   https://www.ncbi.nlm.nih.gov/pmc/articles/PMC2996155/

29   http://annals.org/aim/article-abstract/2653704/patterns-sedentary-behavior-
      mortality-u-s-middle-aged-older-adults

30   https://www.sciencedaily.com/releases/2013/09/130927092350.htm

31   https://www.health.harvard.edu/exercise-and-fitness/the-4-most-important-
      types-of-exercise

32   https://go4life.nia.nih.gov/4-types-of-exercise/

33   https://www.health.harvard.edu/staying-healthy/yoga-benefits-beyond-the-mat

34   https://www.mayoclinic.org/healthy-lifestyle/fitness/in-depth/pilates-for-beginners/art-20047673

35   https://www.betterhealth.vic.gov.au/health/healthyliving/swimming-health-benefits

36   https://www.mayoclinic.org/healthy-lifestyle/fitness/in-depth/ready-to-get-in-on-the-aquatic-fitness-movement/art-20390059

37   https://www.runnersworld.com/beginner/a20847956/6-ways-running-improves-your-health-0/

38   http://content.onlinejacc.org/article.aspx?articleID=1891600

39   http://aje.oxfordjournals.org/content/early/2013/02/27/aje.kws301.full

40   https://www.mayoclinic.org/healthy-lifestyle/fitness/in-depth/strength-training/art-20046670

41   https://www.nerdfitness.com/blog/a-beginners-guide-to-crossfit/

42   https://www.mayoclinic.org/healthy-lifestyle/fitness/expert-answers/zumba/faq-20057883

43   https://www.healthline.com/health/best-core-exercises

44   https://www.stylecraze.com/articles/core-strengthening-exercises

45   https://www.heart.org/en/healthy-living/fitness/fitness-basics/when-is-the-best-time-of-day-to-work-out

46   https://www.unm.edu/~lkravitz/Article%20folder/age.html

47   https://health.gov/paguidelines/second-edition/10things/

48   https://www.healthline.com/health/how-often-should-you-work-out

49   https://www.mentalhealth.org.uk/publications/stress-are-we-coping

50   https://www.hse.gov.uk/statistics/dayslost.htm

51   https://www.physio-pedia.com/Psychological_Basis_of_Pain

52   https://www.ncbi.nlm.nih.gov/pmc/articles/PMC5546756/

53   https://www.ncbi.nlm.nih.gov/pmc/articles/PMC4869967/

54   https://www.ncbi.nlm.nih.gov/pmc/articles/PMC4263906/

55   https://www.takingcharge.csh.umn.edu/what-is-the-mind-body-connection

References

6   World Health Organization. Promoting mental health: concepts, emerging evidence, practice (Summary Report) Geneva: World Health Organization; 2004

7   https://www.sahealth.sa.gov.au/wps/wcm/connect/Public+Content/ SA+Health+Internet/Healthy+living/Healthy+mind/

8   https://www.forbes.com/sites/amymorin/2014/11/23/7-scientifically-proven-benefits-of-gratitude-that-will-motivate-you-to-give-thanks-year-round/

9   https://pubmed.ncbi.nlm.nih.gov/17308390/

0   https://pubmed.ncbi.nlm.nih.gov/25372728/

1   https://pubmed.ncbi.nlm.nih.gov/26972035/

2   https://pubmed.ncbi.nlm.nih.gov/26541426/

3   https://www.hss.edu/conditions_emotional-impact-pain-experience.asp

4   https://time.com/3706692/do-married-people-really-live-longer/

5   https://www.ncbi.nlm.nih.gov/pmc/articles/PMC1449833/

6   https://academic.oup.com/abm/article/35/2/239/4569261

7   https://time.com/5136409/health-benefits-love/

8   https://www.ahajournals.org/doi/full/10.1161/CIR.0b013e31829201e1

9   https://cynthiasass.com/sass-yourself/sass-yourself-blog/item/116-why-you-really-are-what-you-eat.html

0   https://www.ncbi.nlm.nih.gov/pmc/articles/PMC5488800/

1   https://www.hindawi.com/journals/jar/2013/743843/

2   https://medlineplus.gov/ency/article/004012.htm

3   Mitchell HH et al. (1945) The chemical composition of the adult human body and its bearing on the biochemistry of growth. Journal of Biological Chemistry 158(3): 625-37

4   https://www.ncbi.nlm.nih.gov/pubmed/19724292

5   https://www.ncbi.nlm.nih.gov/pubmed/16028566

6   EFSA (2011) Scientific Opinion on the substantiation of health claims related to water and maintenance of normal physical and cognitive functions (ID 1102, 1209, 1294, 1331), maintenance of normal thermoregulation (ID 1208) and "basic requirement of all living things" (ID 1207) pursuant to Article 13(1) of Regulation (EC) No 1924/2006. EFSA Journal 9(4):2075

77   EFSA (2010) Scientific Opinion on Dietary Reference Values for water. EFSA Journal 8(3):1459

78   https://www.ncbi.nlm.nih.gov/pubmed/19724292

79   https://www.ncbi.nlm.nih.gov/pmc/articles/PMC4207053/

80   https://www.dietitians.ca/getattachment/becace49-3bad-4754-ac94-f31c3f04fed0/FACTSHEET-Guidelines-for-staying-hydrated.pdf.aspx

81   https://www.nhs.uk/live-well/alcohol-support/tips-on-cutting-down-alcohol/

82   https://www.naturalhydrationcouncil.org.uk/press/how-hydrated-is-britain/

83   Dr Emma Derbyshire PhD, National Hydration Council, The Essential Guide to Hydration

84   https://www.unlockfood.ca/en/Articles/Water/Facts-on-Fluids-How-to-Stay-Hydrated.aspx

Printed in Great Britain
by Amazon